Once I Was Lost

My Story: Tommy Jituboh

Written by Jeff Jones

Contents

Foreword by Jeff Jones...iv

Acknowledgements...vi

Chapter 1. Early Days..9

Chapter 2. Off the Rails...21

Chapter 3. The Governor..32

Chapter 4. On the Run..51

Chapter 5. H.I.V. Positive...57

Chapter 6. The Grace and Forgiveness of God.......................80

Foreword
by Jeff Jones

I would like to thank Tommy for the trust and belief he had in me by giving me exclusive access into his life, and disclosing some very personal information to enable me to write this enlightening book. There were occasions when I suggested to Tommy that it wasn't necessary to mention things of a personal nature that were unrelated to himself in the book. However, Tommy insisted that he wanted everybody to hear the whole truth as the book is not about his perfection but his direction.

Growing up in the East End, like everyone else I knew the name Tommy Jituboh, who was regarded as a top-ranking villain who wasn't to be messed with. I first met Tommy in 1980 as a 19-year-old while playing football with Berner F.C as an up and coming centre forward. Berner F.C was a young all-black team during a time when there were very few non-blacks in the East End. Match days would attract the racist organisation, the National Front, who shouted racial hatred around the touchline. Their aim was to intimidate us hoping our team would fold, as they felt threatened by our potential and being the only all-black side in the East End. Miraculously, when Tommy joined our team, becoming my striking partner as an experienced 30-year-old, the racism ceased and our young players excelled with confidence, and many went on to play semi-professionally.

The side of Tommy I saw was that of a generous, fearless gentleman who brought people together and broke down racial barriers, becoming a pioneer for Berner F.C and the black community. Tommy led by example, and for the first time gave me a perspective on what true equality feels like, which we achieved while in his company and on the football pitch through the respect shown to us by all races and cultures. This stayed with me throughout my journey. Tommy was one of those characters who everyone in the East End had heard of, with many claiming to know him. However, I had the privilege of being his striking partner and I've never since scored as many goals in a season.

Forty years on, after a career as a manager in mental health, youth work and in education, when I was asked by Tommy to write his autobiography, I was more than happy to oblige as it was a story I felt needed to be heard and which I thoroughly enjoyed writing. What makes this book so intriguing is the honesty that becomes the strength and the social history which reflects the times throughout the journey.

– Jeff Jones

Acknowledgements

I'd like to take this time to give honour to people who have impacted on my life when I became a born-again Christian, as they played a significant part in my journey.

First of all, I would honour my mum and dad who stuck together through thick and thin while bringing up nine children during very deprived times and when racism was blatantly rife. My parents instilled in us the notion of treating people with respect and love. I loved them both very much and I thank God that they were able to see that they got their son back before they died.

Pastor Sonny Senior and Julie Arguinzoni both inspired in me a life change and really influenced me as it was never ever possible for a drug addict to change his life. Sonny was the first person I knew of, so I am grateful to this man and woman of God.

Secondly, to the man, whose name is Art, who spoke to me at King's Cross in 1993 about the love of Jesus. Today, 27 years on, Art is still a part of my life being what we call a spiritual father. If there was an example of gratefulness, I would always point to this man for how God is using his life; I have so much love for this man.

Thirdly, to Bryan and Vivian Villalobos, who became my spiritual parents from the recovery home to the church. Bryan and Vivian were the first pastors who really impacted my life by allowing me to be part of their family and their children. That is where God started to change my understanding of being a father because it was their children that God used. I thank God for this couple and their family who are still a part of my life and whom I visit every time I'm in America. I could go on; however, I'll stop at these three as I know there are many who know what part they played in my recovery.

– Tommy Jituboh

Rock bottom

The13ᵗʰ of July 1993 was another day I woke up hoping that I wouldn't, knowing that my body would be crying for heroin. I was a drug addict, and had been for the last fifteen years, with every day being the same. I was so tired, and I knew that I was going to be sick in my body. As I looked around my flat, there were about fifteen people, male and female, sleeping all over the place and even in my bed. They too were drug addicts, dependent on heroin and cocaine just like myself. Today was going to be so different from yesterday as I had decided to kill myself, as I was sick and tired of the way I was living and I couldn't see any other way out of this misery.

Chapter 1.
Early Days

My name is Tommy Jituboh, and I was born in 1949, the second eldest of nine siblings, five girls and four boys born to Albert and Doreen Jituboh. My father was from Lagos, Nigeria in West Africa and my mother was English from Chelsea. We settled in the East End of London. At seven years old, we moved from Brick Lane to a block called Montefiore Buildings on Cannon Street Road, E1. It had eight apartments on either side and, on the top floor, lived the landlord who collected the rent from the tenants; we called him Mr Montefiore. Mr Montefiore had racing pigeons in the loft which I was fascinated by and I used to go to his home as I couldn't understand why the pigeons returned after being released. Before long, I realised that the pigeons returned to the loft because they got used to that environment, and it was safe so they regarded it as their home. Shortly after, we eventually settled in a council flat on the Berner estate in Welstead House, Cannon Street Road, E1. The estate was inhabited by many large families, mainly white English with a mixture of Asians, Irish, Africans and West Indians. Everyone knew each other and got on OK. We left our front doors unlocked, and if no one was home, you were welcomed into any of your neighbour's flats to wait.

My parents must have had a lot of love for each other to stay together and raise a large family, despite the intense racism of the times. There were many happy times being part of a large family as we had each other for company, to share love, laughter and conversation. When it came to discipline within the household, physical punishment was used, which was common within families during that period. Anything from hairbrushes, pieces of wood, or a leather belt were used by my father on me frequently, especially when I tried to intervene to stop him attacking my mother. My older brother Robbie would always put his arm around me to comfort me, saying, "Don't worry, Tommy, it'll be alright. Dad will stop it soon." Robbie's words always gave me hope and faith that what I was experiencing was just a passing phase and we would soon be a happy family once again.

I was eight years old and weeks would go by where the household was tranquil, although there was always the anticipation at the back of my mind that this was just the calm before the storm. I could sense my dad's moods early in the day, and the rapport he had with my mother before leaving for the gambling house. I would lie in bed awake in the early hours of the morning, before hearing my dad's footsteps slowly walking along the landing and wincing at the sound of the key going into the lock to open the front door. Dad would call my mother in an angry tone of voice, having lost all is money once again. My instincts were right as my father erupted, knocking my mum about before beating me with anything he could get his hands on. Despite me knowing the consequences of my actions for trying to stop an assault on my mother, it would never stop me from trying. Despite my interventions, I would never disrespect my dad as I was afraid of him.

Cannon Street Road was like a playground at the weekends during the 50s as there weren't many cars, and when one did come along, we'd just stop playing either football, tennis or cricket until it drove past. We used to have races from Commercial Road to Cable Street. There were a lot of other activities going on such as cricket and football; it was so much fun. It was a close-knit community where everyone knew each other, so when we got thirsty or hungry, we would go to each other's homes for something to eat or drink. During the summer months, families would be talking to each other from their windows and balconies. I looked forward to Sundays where we would have a lovely roast dinner, and my mum would give us cabbage juice to drink as it was full of iron. Mum was a good cook and would make delicious cakes and Sunday was my favourite day of the week.

There was a place called the Chicken Hill which was a back street that sloped, and we would race our home-made go-karts down it. One day, the kart turned over and one of my mates broke his leg, however, we weren't deterred and continued. On Chicken Hill, there was a place where chickens got slaughtered and my mates and I would go along as spectators as the butchers didn't mind. Every now and again, when their backs were turned, we would cover a chicken with one of our jumpers and steal it and bring it to one of our homes where our parents would cook it for us. Once we stole two large live rabbits from the slaughterhouse and gave them to my mate's dad (a large Maltese man) to cook. He killed them and put them in a huge pot to boil. Moments later, a butcher from the slaughterhouse came marching onto our estate screaming that his prize show rabbits had been stolen and he was offering a reward for their return. We all kept quiet as it was too late and, later that sunny afternoon, we sat at tables and chairs outside in the yard and all the kids ate rabbit stew.

As a young boy, stealing was a real buzz for me. It made me think that I was smart enough to be able to fool adults. It was also a good feeling getting something for nothing as a team, and we now had our own secrets that bonded us as a gang and set us apart from other kids. We began to seek out other opportunities to steal, and we once came across a newspaper stand on

11

Commercial Road where people would take a paper and leave the money when the assistant wasn't around. Our gang would then steal the money and buy sweets and comics, such as the Dandy and the Beano, that came out weekly. I was a very happy child and so were the rest of my family as there was so much excitement. Bonfire Night was something we looked forward to as we would scavenge for wood in derelict buildings and hijack other gang's bonfires. Whoever had the biggest bonfire would have the bragging rights. There were some great memories at that time of my life.

Cannon Street Road was a combination of many cultures with Jewish, Asian and English shop-keepers. The pubs such as The Golden Lion and The British Queen were always heaving with people such as seamen from the docks. There were always fights in the pubs between the locals and the seamen, mainly due to the visitors making a play for the ladies. I was 9 years old the first time I got arrested when our gang ventured to the West End. We used to go to Trafalgar Square where there were swarms of pigeons being fed by tourists. We looked out for racing pigeons that could be identified by the ring around their legs. We would target them by feeding them before grabbing them and taking them home as pets. We were in a park throwing our knives at a tree to see who would be first to get it to stick in. It was then I got arrested by the police for carrying an offensive weapon. I was cautioned and brought home to my parents, where I received one hell of a beating from my father. My dad was very embarrassed having the police arrive at his door with me. Dad came from West Africa and was grateful to be in England, and now his son was showing contempt in the country which had given him an opportunity. That's how Dad saw it and this left him feeling ashamed, as he also felt that my behaviour could be seen as a reflection of his upbringing, which wasn't the case.

Despite my dad being heavy-handed with me for breaking the law, it didn't deter me; it just made me more careful not to get caught. I couldn't understand the embarrassment I was bringing to the family at the time, so I couldn't empathise, as I now had a lust for petty crime and the feeling of euphoria when successful – both of which needed to be fed. From the newspaper stands, we graduated to breaking into gas and electric meters that were situated outside of accommodations. We would go to another area during the times when we expected families to be at work and school, and knock on the doors as a precaution to make sure no one was in. If no one answered, using a screwdriver, we would break the padlocks on the meters, and pour the half crowns (50 pence) into a holdall and head back to our manor and have a carve up (share the money).

It wasn't long before I was frequently getting arrested for stealing and constantly in the Juvenile Court with my mother in tears trying to save me from getting put into care due to my behaviour. I was described in court as a nuisance child. I was now on the police radar and all the local Bobbies knew who I was, so they would stop and search me whenever they saw me. If there was a crime committed and someone of a similar description to myself was flagged up, the police would come for me.

Throughout the East End, there were many derelict buildings that had been bombed during the Second World War. I was 11 years old and Robbie and I use to explore the rubble, building camps and climbing, using it as a playground. We would tie ropes over beams and swing from one derelict room to another, oblivious of the dangers we encountered while filled with excitement. We were forbidden to play in the bombed buildings, so we used to meet there in secrecy and get home before my dad did, so as not to get found out. One day, we didn't get home in time and my dad saw us coming out of the bombed building and gave us a stern warning. "If I find out that youse have been there again you'll get the hiding of your lives." This was one of the first times that I took stock of what my dad had told me. So, instead of following my brother Robbie over to the bombed site, the next day, I went to my local boxing club.

At about 7 pm, I was walking back from the boxing club down Cannon Street Road, when I noticed a huge crowd of people surrounding the bombed building. I enquired of a bystander,

"Hey, mister, what's going on?"

"The building collapsed," he replied, as he pointed to the one we played in. In the mayhem of the crowd and the emergency services' sirens roaring, I couldn't get my head around it. Instinctively, I hurried towards the collapsed building where we used to play and felt somebody grab my arm. I looked behind to see it was my dad. He took me by the hand as we walked the few hundred yards to the hospital in shock and silence, where we joined my mum and sisters. Before long, a doctor came out and pulled my mother aside to have a quiet word. Suddenly, Mum let out a piercing scream like I had never heard before. It wouldn't sink in that my brother had died; even after the funeral, when we laid Robbie to rest, I refused to accept that he was no longer with us. My mother never really got over it.

Soon after, my parents decided to send me to a boarding school in Aldershot, outside of London. I couldn't understand why, although I was reassured that one day I would. I felt a sense of abandonment in the strange environment. There was one other non-white boy, Clarence Carr, who was black and known as a great runner, the best in the school. There were 20 rooms with four sharing a room, and huge playing fields where we played football. Also, we did cross-country running near the moors. On a few occasions, I would abscond from the school and get on the train to Waterloo Station and then get the underground home. My mum would be angry and insist I returned. However, I would go to my friend Terry Tucker's home nearby in Christian Street to hide out for a while, before reluctantly going back. I remained at boarding school from age 11 until I was 14. The day I left that boarding school I was so pleased knowing that I would never have to go back, as the school took me away from the large safe family structure I had been so accustomed to, and introduced me to a group of strangers.

The East End in the 1960s

These were the streets that I was brought up on from the 1950s to the 1970s. It was not too long after the Second World War when the East End of London was bombed, which left many derelict buildings and a diminished workforce due to the lives lost in the conflict. This resulted in a surge of black people recruited by Britain from Africa and the West Indies, 'The Windrush generation', coming to work and build the country back up.

Brick Lane Sunday market

Chapter 2.
Off the Rails

On my return to the East End, I had a friend named Ade who lived on Cable Street, which, in the 1960s, was like a little West End with night clubs and gambling houses where many people would congregate.

Often, it seemed as if the East End had its own laws that the local people lived by. One rule, in particular, was 'Do not grass anybody up to the police' as issues were dealt with internally. For example, if a kid had a fight with another boy and it was a fair match in size and age, there wouldn't be any reprisals. However, if it wasn't a fair match, that was when older brothers or parents would get involved, ensuring the bully was taught a lesson but without the police getting involved. I found myself fighting frequently, mainly due to racist abuse, which I was very sensitive to, triggering an automatic reaction of aggression, despite the size or age of the offending person. I was half-caste (mixed race), both black and white, and saw only equality in the colour of someone's skin and took grave offence at racist abuse, despite it being normalised in those times. I would fight boys many years older than me and never lost a challenge, and before long, racist behaviour seemed to cease in my company, and I began to be accepted within circles of all cultures in the local area. The East End was surrounded by the docks where a lot of stolen goods were for sale within the community. This subsidised the dockers' income by supplying the locals with goods for a third of the price in the shops. To be a thief or to buy stolen goods was the norm in the area and wasn't in the least frowned upon. However, to be a grass or to be seen talking to a policeman would be considered unforgivable.

By the time I was 14 years old, I had very few restrictions from my parents, along with the knowledge that my dad wouldn't hit me anymore or I wouldn't allow it. As a result, I was hardly at home and I spent more time on the streets. I had opted out of education as it didn't mean much to me at the time. I could now do what I wanted to do, so Ade and I drifted into petty crime such as stealing and robbing people.

We were caught up in the bright lights of Cable Street and the lure of independence and acquiring our own money. It was at the tender age of 14 when Ade and I witnessed our first murder in a gambling house. It scared me but didn't stop me from going into those places. Sharing extreme experiences, such as a person being murdered in front of our eyes, bonded Ade and I like brothers as only we shared that memory, and he seemed to fill some of the void left from losing my big brother Robbie. We became inseparable, and, when I wasn't at my home, I was at Ade's home and Ade's mum, Margret, treated me as if I was one of her own sons. My mother would often turn up at Ade's home, confronting Margret for allowing me to spend so much time there, knowing the life I was beginning to lead. My mum would take me home and locked the front door. However, it became a pointless exercise as I would climb out of the window and return to Ade's home. This continued until I was 15 years old.

One night, Ade and I robbed a man in Cable Street, stealing his wallet. It wasn't until two weeks later, whilst walking down Cable Street alone, that I was stopped by the police and taken to Leman St police station. I was told that I was to be taken to see if they could identify me, as I resembled a person involved in an incident of robbery with violence two weeks previously. I was taken to a café in Cable Street and told to sit down in front of a group of elderly people. A white man walked into the room and glared at me, before turning around and walking out. I was then told by the police officer that I was to be charged with robbery with violence.

After spending the night in the police station, I was taken to the local magistrate's courts where I was remanded in custody whilst waiting for my trial to be heard at the Old Bailey. Months later, at the Old Bailey, I was totally unrepresented and the police told lies, however, I pleaded not guilty to all charges. I was found guilty and sentenced to 6-24 months in Borstal, which left me in a daze of confusion. I was sent to Wormwood Scrubs Prison, to a wing for YPs (young prisoners). It was an intimidating place as I was only 15 years old and among inmates up to 5 years older than me. The atmosphere was tense thanks to the testosterone of young men keeping them in anticipation of things kicking off at any given moment. Some of the prison officers (screws) were very unprofessional, to say the least, as they would call us derogatory names to incite a bad reaction in us with the aim of getting YPs into trouble and losing remission for good behaviour. I learnt fast that it was either sink or swim, so I had to adapt and establish myself, just as I did on the streets. However, I was now in a much more dangerous environment as there was no one to turn to or any safe haven. It was relentless with people being bullied, taxed (mugged) and used as joeys (gofers). I decided that I wasn't going to fall into any of those categories as it wasn't in my nature. I made a weapon by melting a toothbrush and setting a razor blade in it.

I had many fights in Scrubs, after which the alarm bells would go off and about 15 screws would come running into the recess (toilets) to break it up. I was then taken to the segregation unit and put into a cell with only a potty until I was hauled in front of the governor. I always pleaded not guilty although I knew I'd be found guilty anyway, and the sentence was usually loss of remission and three days with no food apart from a piece of bread and water. The more often you were in front of the governor, the longer the sentences were, such as 9 days of bread and water, however, there were food interventions between the 9 days. Eventually, I got respect from the other inmates and showed that I was someone not to be messed with.

While in Wormwood Scrubs, waiting to be allocated to Borstal, my dad came to visit me. Dad sat down and pulled out a bar of chocolate and put it on the table and never said one word throughout the 25-minute visit. I could imagine what was going through his mind: "What are you doing with your life?" At the end of the visit, Dad just got up and left and never visited me again. My way of life left my dad feeling so ashamed, he was lost for words. After about a month, I was moved from Scrubs to a Borstal in Wellingborough and put in a unit where every inmate had a single cell. I didn't know anybody, so anyone I spoke to wasn't a friend, they were just an associate. I found Borstal to be a more hostile environment than Scrubs as some Y. Ps had been in there for a while and had formed cliques. New arrivals would then be targeted by predators looking for victims to tax or use as joeys and most hardmen's ambition was to be top dog.

I knew the score from being in Scrubs, so as soon as someone crossed my boundaries, I would let them have it with such a violent rage, inflicting as much damage as possible. The screws would break it up and drag me to my cell while beating me up. As soon as I had the chance, I would steam into them, head-butting, kicking and punching. The screws learned that if they had to come to my cell, they would have to bring plenty of back up and the first few in would be damaged before they eventually restrained me. I found Borstal to be a very dysfunctional environment, much like a gladiator school. It was a place of violence where only the fittest survived and I ensured that I did. I was constantly in some kind of trouble. If I wasn't fighting with an inmate, I was being attacked by the screws (prison wardens) and put in lockdown. Prison is where I learned to become a gladiator as I found myself all alone in the lion's den amongst people who would attack others just because they could. I learned to fight and defend myself; it was then that I vowed I would not allow anyone to put their hand on me, regardless of their size or status.

I ended up losing all my remission and spent much of my time in Borstal in the segregation unit. Most days, the inmates from the segregation unit had to bunny-hop to the gym and were ordered to do a gruelling circuit training, military-style, before bunny-hopping back to our cells. We then had to sit on our chairs and were not allowed to lie on our bed until night time. The inmates on the landings stayed well away from me and I seemed to have made a name for myself due to how defiant I was as a 17-year-old. My sentence was 6 to 24 months and I was released after doing the full amount.

On my release from Borstal at 17 years old, I returned to the East End, to the family home, and linked up with an old friend, Horace Belfont. Horace and I became close friends and back-to-back fighters. My other friend, Ade, had now become a heroin addict and I found out that Ade and his girlfriend had both received 5 years in prison for selling heroin in Greek Street in the West End of London. I had no contact with Ade as I wasn't into drugs. I was now into clubbing with my best pal Horace and we could both handle ourselves in fights. My biggest weapon was my head and I used to get in first with an enormous headbutt, which always did the job and never let me down.

Horace's secret weapon was his cut-throat razor, which was an accessory that he never left home without. Horace did a lot of damage to many people and soon had a reputation and was known as Horace the Cutter - those who weren't his friends avoided him.

Growing up in the East End, there were not a lot of activities you could take part in, so many young people hung around in gangs. There were gangs from Wapping, Mile End, and Canning Town, however, my gang from Cannon Street Road were the firm. As up and coming teenagers, we used to go to clubs such as the A-Train in Mile End, which often ended with fights against the bouncers that we always won. This was due to our general dislike of authority. On one occasion, the bouncers were hesitantly and politely trying to ban us from entering the club due to the previous turnouts. Things were becoming heated, when the owner came out, called us aside and said, "Listen, lads, I'll let youse in for nothing on condition you stop beating up our bouncers." We agreed and had no problem there after that. We would also go to a club in Ilford called the Grotto and pubs such as Black Boy, The Blind Beggar and The King's Head. We were into Motown and reggae music and looked forward to Notting Hill carnival in West London once a year. I had the talent to become a professional footballer, however, talent is nothing without discipline. My reputation let me down and I was deemed as bad influence due to the name I had on the Streets, I believe that is why football clubs stayed away from me.

The sixties were a time of a lot of racial unrest, with the civil rights movement being established. This led to the emergence of black power organisations such as the Black Panthers in America and liberators like Martin Luther King, Malcolm X, Rosa Parks and Angela Davis. The movement raised awareness and had a big influence in the UK, as it swept through the inner cities. There were huge campaigns highlighting black pride, encouraging black people to love themselves, after many centuries of their culture being demonised. This empowered black youths to embrace their identity and many began wearing their hair in huge afros and cane rows and forming their own communities. They would organise their own parties at home or in halls, with huge handmade sound systems where all cultures were welcomed. I grew up at a time where racism was blatantly condoned with signs in houses with rooms for rent that read, "No blacks, no Irish or dogs allowed". We were very frustrated and we had a very low tolerance when it came to racial abuse. Horace and I were up and coming, emerging as a force to be reckoned with on the streets and we couldn't be stopped. Despite there being a lot of racism, I grew up with a lot of white friends who I was very close to and we fought together against racism. I was never a racist; I just didn't accept it.

One early morning, after the clubs in the West End had closed, Horace and I went to an illegal drinking club in North London known locally as a Shebeen or Blues dance. One had to be familiar with the doorman or you needed to know a regular to gain access for a fee of one pound. The premises were usually packed with people, and it had a bar and a sound system called 'Suckle' with massive speakers pumping out soul and reggae music. I was 19 years old and I was getting on fabulously, dancing with a very attractive blonde woman who was about 30 years old. At that time, I had never had a girlfriend before and it felt like I had just won the pools. Suddenly, a Jamaican man stepped in front of us, having heated words with the woman. I was bemused at what was going on, when all of a sudden, he pulled out a knife and cut her across her breast. He then turned to me and, instinctively, I head-butted him, knocking him to the floor and out cold. The place was packed. Horace clocked what was going on from the bar and pulled out his razor, racing through the crowd, swinging his hand from left to right like he was cutting through dense bushes, and in the process, severally cut about eight of the mob which was echoed by their screams of terror.

The music had stopped playing, and Horace and I moved from the centre of the dance floor backing on to the rear wall as a precaution, to ensure our attackers couldn't get us from behind. We slowly moved forward like wild animals preparing to fight for our lives. To our surprise, the crowd began to back off as we hovered slowly forward. The place was like a blood bath and, to our astonishment, the main door was thrust open inviting us to leave. As the cold air swept in and the police sirens roared outside, Horace and I slipped away from the scene unmarked. The Jamaican was known in the hood as Vicious with a fearsome reputation and Horace and I went on his turf and caused so much damage without any reprisals. It was now that we had a reputation as famous 'top-ranking' street fighters.

Due to the lifestyle I was living, I was breaking my mother's heart as she feared losing her other son, this time to the streets. I would always offer my mum money and she always refused to accept anything, and would say, "I never raised you like that." That was true but I had so much anger and frustration within myself and no one I could talk to about it, so I would do what I had to do. My mum and I seemed to have a special bond, although she loved me no more than any of my other siblings. From the time I came out of Borstal, my dad hardly spoke to me because of the person I was becoming. I didn't really have a relationship with my father; we never discussed my lifestyle or the morality surrounding the choices I was making.

I really believed that Dad was trying to find his own place in England, coming from West Africa and trying to integrate into a completely different culture where he had very few contacts. It was difficult, unlike for the indigenous population who were already settled with an extended family structure for support. My dad's top priority was to work, work and work to provide for his family, and the racism he had to contend with manifested itself in the frustration that was vented in the home. I know my dad loved me in his own way, however, he found it difficult to express it, especially with someone as defiant as myself. We just couldn't see eye to eye as nobody could tell me at the time that how I was living was wrong; it felt right to me, due to the respect I received on the streets.

Horace and I were making our own money from armed robberies of security vans, and from companies delivering and collecting money from banks. We would get tip-offs from maybe someone working in a large factory who didn't get on with the boss. They knew where, when and at what time someone would go to the bank to collect the money to pay the staff. Horace and I would be waiting in the back of a stolen transit van, spying through small holes that were drilled through the back doors. When we saw the boss, who was usually accompanied by a member of staff walking close by, we would burst out of the van and snatch the cash before driving off. We always gave a drink (money) to the person who tipped us off.

When it came to robbing banks, we used to watch from the back of a transit van to establish what time the armoured vans would arrive to deliver the money. On the day of the robbery, there would usually be four of us; one person stayed in the driver's seat and the rest of us, wearing balaclavas, would hold up the security guards with guns before they went into the bank. We knew the protocol that the security guards were instructed not to retaliate during an armed raid, and we always got the money without a struggle. We would then drive away before switching to another vehicle. The most we ever stole on one robbery was £100,000 which was a huge amount back then. Unlike today, they didn't have dye-packs installed in cash boxes that would be activated if stolen, destroying all the banknotes inside.

The proceeds were spent living the high life, which was our passion - clubbing and clothes. We loved to dress slick and we were given top respect on the manor which was a positive thing to me, so how could anybody make me see that I was wrong? I believed that what I had was what most people in life had strived for - respect. I would go home with wads of money and my mother refused to accept any of it. She didn't want to encourage my involvement in crime; like most parents, they didn't want their children in jail. They just hoped that the 'penny would drop' soon and my behaviour would change.

During those times, Horace and I felt untouchable as we had all the time in the world. Since a robbery was only necessary every so often, we lived a nice lifestyle, clubbing most nights, unlike the average man who worked 40-hour weeks, with the highlight being a night out at the local pub. I was becoming a very radical and frustrated young man. Although I wasn't heavily into drugs, on occasions, I took pills called purple hearts, which were popular in the 60s; it was a type of speed. My real buzz was being a villain, living outside of the law and thinking outside of the box. It was then that I felt free in mind, body and soul as I was my own man. I didn't have to suck up to a boss whom I depended on to put food on my table. I thought for myself and I did what I wanted to do. I could drink in any pub in the East End and, being the only non-white, there wouldn't be a problem. That, to me, represented freedom and independence and was when I was in my element. People began to call me The Governor.

To establish myself and to gain the title in the East End as The Governor involved many fights to make my mark in the 50s and 60s. My reasons for being a violent fighter and never losing a fight was due to the fear of the violence my dad used on me and I never wanted to experience that again. It was so terrifying that every time I confronted someone in a fight, that fear would come into my mind and make me win. I wouldn't allow anybody to make me feel that fear again. I often fought and that's how I became known as The Governor as I was feared on the streets.

Chapter 3.
The Governor

If anyone indulged in class 'A' drugs on the streets at the time, we considered them to be a liability or a police informer, as that was considered a sign of weakness, and they were seen as people who would sell their soul for a fix. I was a villain whose passion was clubbing, cars, clothes, women and violence, so we stayed away from class 'A' drug users, as we had little in common with them. With the proceeds of our robberies, we would get dressed up and head down the West End. One of our haunts was a club called The Roaring 20s, that was a black club that hosted many top celebrities, and was strictly invitation only. I could turn up randomly, fifteen-handed and gain access from the bouncers, as I was well known and highly respected due to my lifestyle. I had only ever been beaten by one man before, and that was my father, and that fact still remains true today.

At the age of 21, I was seen as a form of celebrity to some people and when we were in the clubs, we were left alone. One morning, after a night at The Roaring 20s, me and a close friend, Micky Stermy, went to a late-night drinking club in Greek Street, which was a bit of a dive. Micky got into an argument with four men and a fight erupted, so I steamed in, punching into them and ended up in a doorway when somebody shut the door on us. I knew we had to get out as there were too many of them and Micky was on the floor. I opened the door and pulled Micky out of harm's way on to the street. There was a lot of commotion with a circle of people shouting and screaming. We were confronted by this huge white man with an Alsatian dog on a lead, barking furiously whilst snapping at us. I pulled out a knife and stabbed the dog in the head which made the dog back off, then we took off in the other direction, before getting a taxi back to the East End.

The next day, the incident was on the news. They announced that one of the men in the club was a plainclothes policeman, who suffered a broken nose, and his police dog was stabbed. The police came looking for us in the East End but arrested someone who looked like me. Before long, I was arrested, but I don't know if my name was put up by the person arrested first. My mother's sister's husband, Uncle Tommy, was a villain and gave a detective on the case a bung (some money), so he lessened the charges, resulting in my case not going for trial at the Crown Court and I was treated leniently. That incident against a policeman raised my profile as a public enemy, and I was frequently accosted by the police and pulled into their vans and beaten up. On one occasion, I was strangled to the point that I passed out, and they tried to fit me up for crimes I didn't commit; they wanted me off of the street at any cost. When I was attacked by the police in the cells, I always made sure that they knew they were in a fight and injured them while defending myself on many occasions.

There were always women around us and I had many relationships. I wasn't loyal to one lady at a time, and they knew it, although I would not throw it in their faces. I could sleep with a different woman every day of the week if I wanted to, however, they weren't what I would describe as love relationships. The women were infatuated with villains and their lifestyles of shopping, nice cars, clubs, money, jewellery and the free time we had. This also meant that we were very flexible and could meet up at any given time. One lovely summer's evening, I was at an East End festival with my mates when a young lady approached me and said, "My friend Pauline likes you." She was pointing to a very attractive mixed-race lady, whose family I was familiar with. 'Wow, she's nice,' I thought. So, I went over for a chat with Pauline before leaving, as I had arrangements that night to go clubbing. As I was getting ready at home, someone whistled outside. I looked out of the window to see a bloke who shouted, "Pauline's here and she just wants to say good night." "Ask her to come up," I yelled. Pauline came up and we talked for a while and had a kiss and agreed to meet up later that week. Pauline left while I went out clubbing with my firm.

For the next couple of months, Pauline and I saw each other regularly and I really got to like her, although I didn't love her; it was not that I didn't want to, it was more that I was in love with the lifestyle I was living. I cared for Pauline and I made sure that she was looked after but I would make up excuses that I had to be elsewhere, and be out with my friends and with other women, which wasn't unusual in my world. Pauline announced that she was pregnant and I was thrilled to bits with the thought of becoming a father. I tried very hard to tone down my lifestyle. Pauline gave birth to a boy on the 15th of July 1974. We named him Jermyn and we celebrated with family and friends in our local pub, The King's Head. A few months later, I got arrested for something and Pauline found out that I was involved in another relationship with a lady, Tracy from Bow. While spending time in prison, Pauline didn't want anything to do with me, however, we got back together on my release but things just weren't the same as I was married to my lifestyle.

I was in a club in the West End when I was approached by a beautiful lady who introduced herself as Trina and she asked me if I could help her out as she was being bullied by a bloke called Roy. Trina lived in a lovely affluent area in Marble Arch. I told her to get Roy to go to her flat and, once inside, to give me a call and I would deal with it. After receiving the call, me and a friend, Ralph, went to Trina's flat. "Where is he?" I whispered.

"Upstairs," she mimed while pointing her index finger upwards.

"Wait here, Ralph," I said as I slowly walked upstairs.

Laying on the bed, there was a huge West Indian bloke about 6 foot 4 inches tall. I got very close to him before he noticed me and I said "Oi!! What ya doing? Don't you move!" I could see the fear on his face as he gripped the blankets and froze on the spot. I went on to say, "Trina is with me, so listen carefully as I won't repeat myself, and if I hear that you have been in contact with Trina in any way or form, you'll be sorry, believe me, as I mean what I say. It's your lucky day as I'm in a good mood so, I'll give you a chance to leave in one piece." He got up, scrambling to his feet, and left. I happened to see him again in a club in the West End, The Roaring 20s, when he was with about 10 of his mates, and when I walked in with Trina and my firm, he walked out, never to be seen or heard from again. Trina became my girlfriend. It wasn't love; we were just infatuated with each other. Trina was financially independent so I didn't have to support her although she did suggest that I gave up my runnings so she could support me. However, that wasn't me. I didn't live off women; I was content doing my robberies and making my own monies.

Eventually, Trina moved into my flat with me in the East End and my son, Clark, was born. After about a year, I ended up in prison and on my release, I went back to live with Trina and Clark but the relationship had run its course so we went our separate ways.

There were huge changes in the East End during the 70s, as it was now apparent that there was a culture that caused a divide between the police and locals. This came to light after the trial of a notorious crime family who ruled the underworld and lived only a mile from Cable Street. It was then discovered that the East End had its own culture that included a wall of silence, which made it extremely difficult for the police to solve crime in the area, as residents refused to come forward in fear of reprisals. There was a vagrant with one leg who roamed the East End on crutches, and kids would throw rotten tomatoes at him, calling him "Grass", as it was rumoured that his leg was amputated by a crime family for grassing them up, so he was left as an example in the community. It was incidents like this that instilled fear into people and demonstrated the risk involved in being an informer.

After several years, my luck began to run out, probably due to our naivety of believing we could maintain our lifestyles without any accountability whatsoever. People in the community talked and got jealous and, before long, we became suspects of the police surveillance team. As a result, I received a four-year prison sentence. On reflection during my time in jail, I thought that with all the money I was earning through crime, I should have set up a business as a front, to give people the impression that I worked hard for my lifestyle, which may have kept me under the radar. Having a business as a front was what many criminals started to do, due to the change of culture in the East End, where 'grassing' was now becoming socially acceptable.

During my time in prison, I had numerous fights, mostly earlier on. It was like gladiators fighting for survival, and I became much more violent, using my head and my fists. I became established as a top-ranking violent prisoner, never ever losing a fight. Before long, because of my reputation, I rarely needed to fight in prison; only on the odd occasion when new arrivals came on to my wing and crossed my boundaries, I had to put them in their place.

That seemed to be my life as a villain, bank robber and a violent criminal, as where could I go from now? There was no turning back as I had followed my dream and my role models such as the Kray twins, the Richardson's, the Dixon's, the Blundell's and the Nash's. They were all top villains and I wanted to aspire to their level. Being a villain for me was more than just having money, it was about being accepted during a very racist period, where I witnessed white people spitting at my mother while calling her a 'nigger lover.' Also, I witnessed my father leaving for work each morning, concealing a weapon as a deterrent if racially attacked, when he wasn't naturally that way inclined. However, these were dangerous times and I refused to accept that type of behaviour from anyone. So, the attraction of being a villain was magnified, as my reputation would not only protect me and give me respect, it would also protect my family. I was now the eldest sibling with five sisters to look out for. My reputation wasn't always welcomed within the family because, as my sisters got older, as attractive as they were, it was very difficult for them to go on dates once their potential boyfriends realised that I was their brother.

I came out of prison unafraid of anybody and a radical young man, as I knew how it felt to be respected by everyone as a half-caste man while in prison, and nothing less would now be acceptable. The East End was changing rapidly with a lot of development taking place throughout Wapping, Aldgate and the Isle of Dogs (The Docklands). Many commercial and residential properties were being built, resulting in an influx of middle-class people moving into the East End, who were referred to as 'Yuppies.' A racist organisation, calling themselves the National Front, emerged, who would go on rallies and, in groups, would distribute leaflets on racial hatred through letterboxes on local housing estates. They would terrorise lone non-white people when in a gang. Horace and I were appalled at the thought of these thugs from the National Front encroaching on our manor. As far as I was concerned, the propaganda they were distributing could influence a racist attack on my family and I couldn't sit back and watch it happen.

There was a place in London called the 'White House' where radical black people would congregate influenced by the Black Panther Party in America. The Black Panther Party (BPP) was founded in 1966 in Oakland, California, by college students, Huey P. Newton and Bobby Seale. It was a revolutionary organisation formed during the civil rights movement as self-defence for black people under attack. After receiving tip-offs on the manor of where the National Front were distributing their leaflets, me, Horace and our associates would ambush the racists, with Horace using his trademark cut-throat razor and me my head and fist. I now felt that I was giving something back to the community and I was part of the solution rather than the problem. I now felt that I was putting my violent behaviour to good use, not just to line my pockets. I now felt that I was a villain with a cause.

One of my passions was playing football in which I always participated in prison. I would describe myself as an old-fashioned centre forward; I was good in the air, holding up play, unsettling the defence while scoring my fair share of goals. I heard of the emergence of a talented all-black young football team on the manor called Berner United, who were turning over some of the established teams in the league. I was made aware that Berner United were being targeted at matches by the National Front, who would flock around the pitch shouting racial abuse and threatening violence. I sent a white friend of mine to blend into the crowd one match day to clock if he recognised faces who were part of the National Front. I was infuriated at the feedback that I had received and the abuse Berner United had to tolerate on and off the pitch. Even the referee wasn't generous with his decision-making due to the intimidation. The average age of Berner United was 20 years old but they were playing against 30-year-old, big, unforgiving men and only had their talent to do the talking to win the game, as they were no physical match for their opposition. They were also outnumbered by their army of racist thugs on the side-line.

I was hurt from the report that I received of how black people were being treated in the East End, when they represented only a fraction of the local population. I grew up on the Berner Estate where people feared to tread, so I arranged a meeting through the manager, Stephen Ballen, for the whole team to join me for a drink in my local, the Crown & Dolphin on Cable Street. The squad turned up - there were the Clarkes, Phillips, Tucker, the Willers, Gorden and Jones, to name a few. The team were made up of tradesmen and hustlers. Before introducing myself, I put a wad of cash in a pint glass on the bar and told the team they could drink as much as they wanted. Unsurprisingly, they had all heard of me but didn't know me personally as I was about 10 years older than the average player. I proposed that I wanted to play for Berner United which was welcomed by all.

I was so excited at the prospect of playing for Berner United on a Sunday morning, as it made me feel normal being among everyday people and sharing the banter and love for a few hours a week. I could be myself and remove all of my barriers and personas for a while before returning to life in the jungle for the rest of the week. I was playing in my familiar target-man role with Jeff Jones and Curtis Phillips on either side of me. The way I played and my presence on the pitch became contagious throughout the team, who began to come of age, adding a lot more steel to their game. More importantly, the National Front did not turn up at any of the matches and Berner United were giving as good as they got on the pitch while winning games convincingly.

Berner United were playing a cup match against another all-black team from Hackney over the Marshes when it started to get a bit naughty with hard tackles flying in. Our centre half, Joey, and their striker started exchanging punches, erupting into a full-scale war, leaving the official running off the park. There were players swinging their football boots above their heads by the laces, using them as weapons, and flag poles being used as spears during the mass brawl. If this had taken place when I was with my firm, I would have led the fight due to my loyalty to my mates. However, I now saw things differently and saw the bigger picture as the older and wiser man, with my influence enabling me to stop the chaos. I shouted at the top of my voice, "This is Tommy. Everybody, stop now." Everyone did, standing there like statues. Wagging my finger, I demanded that the two who had triggered the brawl come to me; they walked over like naughty schoolboys about to be told off, while both squads looked on. I said, "This is so sad; you are all talented black footballers and the minority in the area and look at youse fighting against each other, which will only divide you even more in the future and not unite youse." I asked Joey and the centre forward if they had a personal problem, then suggested they should have a straightener (one on one) and I would make sure that nobody jumped in. They both agreed.

A huge ring was formed and the two of them steamed into each other while being cheered by the other players. After about five minutes of fighting, the exhausted duo was wrestling and throwing lame punches. I intervened and told the two of them to stop and shake hands, which they did, and both teams left the field in harmony. I was asked afterwards by the players why I had used that approach of letting the two people have a straightener when were a firm and should fight together. I said, "You need to have your own mind and be able to think for yourself without letting just loyalty dictate how you behave or who you mix with. If you don't, you could allow any little runt to lead you to trouble which is nothing to do with you, or you don't even agree with. You'll end up in the hot seat and the instigator can walk away scot-free. As men, you should fight your own battles without causing a war. This was just a football match; if the fight wasn't stopped, who knows what the outcome would have been? Someone could have been killed and others ending up doing life in prison, all for what?" I felt it was my duty to protect and educate the players, although I wouldn't have used that approach in my world as it would have been seen as a sign of weakness. I didn't want to encourage these young players to become who I was, a villain, as I was in too deep and couldn't turn back. I began to wish I could live an ordinary life. I think the penny was beginning to drop, and this was the first sign of spiritual awakening that I felt just needed to be unlocked.

I so looked forward to Sundays, playing football for Berner and being part of such a talented side, as we were sitting at the top of the division and were now rarely losing a match. I hardly missed a game, although, most of the time, I arrived straight from raving and the worse for wear. Unlike on the street where I was known as The Governor, among my teammates, I was just Tommy and I felt protective in the form of a father figure as I was 10 years older than the average player. I had to prove myself on the pitch, week in and week out, to keep my shirt just like everyone else. It was more than just winning a football match to us as we were playing for pride, and to prove that the only black team in the East End were among the best and we feared no one. My teammates and I became friends and I would invite them to my house parties where there were always free drinks and a bowl of top-grade marijuana for my guests. I would also treat the team to nights out in clubs in the West End, insisting that they left their wallets at home, as the night was on me.

That season, Berner United won the league and cup double, so, as a treat, I asked the team to meet me in The Crown and Dolphin as I would be taking them out to celebrate on me. After a good drink, I ordered taxis that took us to a club in Dalston. I knew the bouncers who let us all in and I put some money behind the bar and told the lads to drink all they wanted. The night was going well and we were in high spirits, reflecting on our season, when suddenly, six smartly dressed men walked in and stood by the bar. I saw red as I had some unfinished business with three of the men. Once in that frame of mind, I don't see logic such as 'I'm outnumbered so why not leave it for another day'. I can't help but deal with it there and then. Instinctively, I approached a friend of mine who was built like a bodybuilder and whispered in his ear. He then went over to a fruit machine, grabbed it in a bear hug and put it down in front of the entrance, blocking the access. I stood opposite the men, staring at them. On recognising me, they froze with their eyes opened wide. I don't know why but I ripped off my shirt and let out an almighty roar, steaming bare-backed into the group, head-butting the first two before my fists were flying at the rest of them. A few of the men quickly dispersed, heading to the exit, only to find it blocked by the fruit machine. Then all hell was let loose in the club with a massive brawl. Bouncers eventually arrived, clearing the doorway and allowing a couple of the men left standing to escape.

I played for Berner United for one season only and felt that I had contributed towards putting them on the map. They were a young side and, as they matured, they became a dominant team in East London, winning many honours. A few years later, after winning the double yet again, seven of the team were signed up to a semi-professional team, Slade Green, who played in the Kent league. After rebuilding the team, Berner United went on to establish themselves as a top side for many years.

Berner F.C 1980s

A day out with my son Clarke 1976

Me and Trina with my family 1978

My local, The Crown & Dolphin 1980

Family 1982

The 3rd generation

Family

Me and Nicky 1982

*1984 - on the run after escaping from police custody &
having to saw the handcuffs off.*

Chapter 4.
On the Run

I was alerted by my mother that the police were looking for me for an armed robbery that I had recently committed. I decided to go on the run and headed straight to my uncle's home in Chelsea, as he had helped me out in the past. Uncle Tommy offered me a room at his house, which I declined, as I felt I had to make my own way, however, I welcomed any future advice. I got to know a West Indian bloke, Jubby. He was the sort of person you go to in the area if you needed anything done, and I ended up staying under wraps (hidden) in his flat on a huge estate called the World's End. There were a lot of different people coming and going from Jubby's flat, and that was when I was introduced to an attractive mixed-race girl named Nicky. Nicky was 23 years old, 10 years younger than me and before long, we became lovers and inseparable. I knew that Jubby was part of the drug culture and assumed that Nicky smoked a bit of dope; it was only when I moved into her flat with her on the estate that I was hit with the bombshell that Nicky was a heroin addict.

My initial reaction was to get the hell out of there, as it was a habit that I detested and something that I couldn't understand, and I kept well away from that type of people. This was different as I liked Nicky a lot and I believed that I could help her to get off heroin. The more I tried to help Nicky, the more frustrated I became, as I learnt that addicts are expert liars. There were times when I thought we were winning and then discovered that the person I'd been trying to help was secretly still consuming heroin while in the toilet, and that brought me to the end of my tether. I wasn't in a good place myself, having been on the run now for a couple of months, and unable to contact my family or friends in East London. My support wasn't working and Nicky was struggling, so, as a last-ditch attempt, I said,

"If you're on heroin, I'll get on it also, as I'd rather you be upfront with me than do it behind my back."

"Tommy, are you crazy? You don't know how addictive heroin is."

"Look, Nicky, let's take some together now, and then, when we decide to come off it, we can both do it together, as we'll both be in the same boat."

Nicky injected me and my mind was all over the place before crashing out. I came round in the morning with Nicky holding my hand, and told me that I had OD'd (over-dosed). I felt that I had slept well for the first time in months and all my problems had disappeared. That is what I liked about heroin; it took away the worry of being on the run and going back to prison for a while, before being stalked by my problems again and needing another hit. I began to enjoy escaping and experimented mixing heroin with cocaine and vitamin C, where it would go dark brown while my girl injected me. Before I knew it, my life revolved around heroin and I couldn't do without it. My money was now running out, and I wasn't in the state of mind to do an armed robbery on a bank or building society, as that took time and patience to plan which I never had any more. My priority was to get quick cash to feed my heroin addiction, because I couldn't even think coherently, as I was now an addict.

I linked up with my old friend, Ade, who had been sentenced to five years in prison, along with his girlfriend, for dealing heroin in the West End. Ade now, coincidently, lived on the World's End Estate, a few floors above Nicky and I. We targeted drug dealer's homes with masks covering our faces, then, once inside, we would brandish weapons, demanding the drugs and the money and using violence if necessary. This method was quicker easier money; besides, the drug dealers wouldn't go to the police, so there was no chance of getting arrested. We would also get tip-offs on couriers who had just smuggled class 'A' drugs into the country, who we would also rob. We ended up keeping more drugs than we sold as that's all I seemed to do, consume drugs. Eventually, I began losing my self-respect as I wasn't taking care of myself and adapting to a low standard of hygiene. Life wasn't about waking up in the morning anymore, having a nice breakfast, then a shower while taking my time ironing my clothes to perfection. The only thing that mattered was my next fix. As soon as my eyes were opened, my first reaction was to look for the spoon and prepare my first fix of the day, injected by Nicky.

Heroin was like a sleeping drug and cocaine was like a high rush. One took you down and the other took you up. This was my life as a drug addict and I was declining by the day and rapidly losing weight. I deteriorated so much in six months. Prior to then, when I bought clothes, I would buy the best in a shop called Cecil Gees. If you had money, that's where you went and that's how I lived as a villain. Six months on, I was now a junkie, trapped, unable to break free and regretfully succumbing to class 'A' drugs. My sisters would come looking for me and cry, saying, "Tommy, what are you doing to yourself?" I would pretend I was fine and then lie to them that I needed money to pay my rent, which they gave me as they loved me as their big brother. They would tell me that they had heard rumours that I was a heroin addict which I would always deny.

One night, my little sister Julie had a dream that I was in trouble and contacted the rest of my siblings who all came over to Nicky's flat in Chelsea. I wasn't in so Nicky gave them Ade's address a few floors up and said I was there. They pressed the lift and, to their horror, when the lift door opened, I was lying on the floor of the lift as I had overdosed. They called the ambulance and, on my way to the hospital, I almost swallowed my tongue. Once in hospital, they put electrics on me as my heart had stopped beating for about a minute, and I was brought back to life. I came around with all my family around me, and I strongly denied that my condition was due to overdosing on heroin and was due to being drunk, which put them in two minds. I was released from hospital that night and my family made sure I was comfortable and tucked up in bed at the flat before returning to the East End. As soon as I saw their taxis leave the block from our window, Nicky and I went out to score some heroin.

I was technically dead a few hours before and there I was buying heroin. I was a slave to the drug as it took control of my life. It was at that point that I began to realise there was no hope for me to get out of this devastating situation. The only way out was to die a drug addict, or to go back to prison, spending the rest of my life in there. I was now barely surviving and, most days, I felt so sick with no money, crying out for heroin. As I got deeper into the addiction, my enemies saw it as an opportunity to take me out. As a result, and for the first time in my life, I made sure I had a serious weapon with me at all times. As I was so skinny, if I had to head-butt someone, I would have probably knocked myself out. The people I was now running with were low-life, with some who would sell their own granny for a fix. Not so long ago, I wouldn't have given this company the time of day, and now I needed these people as a source of survival as I was now in their category.

My future looked bleak and I saw no hope, as I now knew people who had been trying for years to get clean and had been in and out of rehab. On release, they went straight back on the gear. I now believed:

"Once a drug addict always a drug addict."

At 5 am on a Monday, as I lay in bed writhing in pain and vomiting into a bucket, the front door came crashing in and I heard the shouts of "Police, don't move." The bedroom door was flung open and Nicky screamed as about 10 armed police swarmed around the bed. I was handcuffed and taken to the police station and then to court the next day where I was remanded in custody. I was so sick with withdrawal symptoms from the drugs, however, that for the first time in my life, going to prison was welcomed as I would now not be around as much heroin, which may have given me time to get clean.

I received a 3-year sentence and went to Wandsworth prison in South London which had a reputation of being a racist prison. I witnessed wardens holding down black inmates while cutting off their dreadlocks. One morning, when queuing up at the hotplate for breakfast, I saw a black guy, who looked very familiar, serving the food. He looked back at me and said,

"Tommy."

"I know I know you but I can't place you," I said.

"I'm Clarence Carr from boarding school."

"Oh!! Of course! How long are you doing, Clarence?"

"Life, for murder."

"Wow, I copped a three; we'll catch up." I walked on as I was holding up line. I haven't seen Clarence since.

Before long, I was transferred to Rollingstone prison to serve the remaining of my sentence. The prison was near Stonehenge and was used many years before as a concentration camp, so there were soldiers on the four corners with guns.

Although I was still taking drugs inside, it was not nearly as much as I was doing when I was out. I was eating regularly, exercising and getting back to my fighting weight. One morning, in the workshop, a friend of mine, Steve McGuiness, was having an argument with a few inmates which escalated into a fight. I steamed in, decking two of them. The screws were terrified and froze while a few more headed towards me and Steve. The fighting commenced as I knocked someone out with my trademark head-butt. The alarm sounded and loads of screws burst into the workshop. Steve and I were dragged away with blood all over us and placed in lockdown. The incident resulted in Steve being shipped out to Parkhurst on the Isle of Wight and I was given an extra 190 days on top of the 3-year sentence I was serving.

Six months later, there was a riot in the prison with the prisoners taking over the building. There I was on the rooftop, ripping the slates off and throwing them like boomerangs across the yard. This went on for about a week before order was restored. The riot had caused £3.6 million worth of damage which was a huge amount of money at the time. I was given another 6 months on top of my sentence. I was beginning to think I would never get out; however, I was eventually released in 1988.

Chapter 5.
H.I.V. Positive

I was eventually released from prison in 1988 after serving the whole 3-year sentence with no remission for good behaviour. I promised myself that I would never go back to prison again, as I had been fighting two wars; crime and drug addiction. I was losing on both counts and it just didn't make sense. I returned to the East End with my family, intent on doing the right thing this time around. I didn't get in touch with my ex-girlfriend, Nicky, as I wanted to stay away from the temptation of drugs.

Being off the manor for so many years, I had noticed a lot of changes with the regeneration and the working class and yuppies (middle class) were now integrated. Due to the introduction of Margaret Thatcher's policy of the 'Right to Buy', it gave council tenants the opportunity to purchase their property at a huge discount. Many of the locals took advantage of the Right to Buy scheme, buying and then selling their council properties, making a huge profit and migrating to Essex. The amount of investment poured into the East End increased property prices in the area phenomenally, with the value of a small council flat worth more than a large house with a garden outside of London. This appealed to many local people who saw it as an opportunity to move off the council estates. As a result, the yuppies moved into the East End in droves and were now buying council properties as they were close to their jobs in the City. This had a huge effect on the dynamics in the East End as I never knew whether our new neighbours were Old Bill (police) or not.

I found myself at a total loss as the people I knew had moved on with their lives and settled down with families, some working in normal jobs and others were doing time. Even being a criminal was now a huge challenge as there were C.C.T.V cameras everywhere, when back in the day, they were only used in banks. There were now cameras on nearly every street corner. Many criminals had now turned their attention to drug dealing with the class 'A' drugs now flooding the street, and the emergence of junkies. I felt totally ostracised from society and felt as though I didn't fit in, and eventually, gave in to the urge and visited Nicky in Chelsea. Nothing much had changed with Nicky; she was still a drug addict with her life revolving around scoring a fix. I didn't have the discipline, strength or will to resist and I ended up back on the gear straight away and resuming our relationship, as, deep down, I did love her.

One morning, after our first fix, Nicky said,

"Tommy, I want you to go to the hospital for a check-up."

Frowning and confused, I looked at Nicky and replied,

"Hospital? What on earth for?"

"Just do it for me, babe," replied Nicky.

After the check-up, I was given the bombshell that I was H.I.V. positive and I had caught the virus through sharing needles while injecting drugs. I held my head in my hands in devastation thinking that I had just received a death sentence. I went home to Nicky with the news, to discover that not only was she also H.I.V. positive but she was pregnant with my baby. Nicky and I began arguing like nothing before blaming each other, as we both feared bringing a child into the world just to die of H.I.V. along with the parents. In the late 1980s, there was no cure or medication for H.I.V. and most people infected died, so we knew where we were destined. I knew that we were dying; it was only a matter of time.

I stopped doing drugs with Nicky and I began using with other people. The strain on our relationship was relentless, to say the least, resulting in Nicky and I splitting up. I headed to King's Cross, a red-light district in London at the time, where prostitutes, pimps, drug dealers and stowaways congregated. It was like a melting pot of people just waiting to die. I made my presence felt on the streets (knocking) taking drugs from dealers and not paying them. I still had my reputation going for me, so I feared no reprisals. I was at such a low ebb with phenomenal problems to contend with, so all the greater was the desire to escape from it all. Although I hated the life I was living, I didn't know or see any way out of it. Drugs were the king that now ruled my life and the only way to free myself from my hell was to kill myself.

A friend, Peter, who I use to inject with on the Streets of King's Cross, went missing for a while. When this happened, it was assumed among the Street community that the person was either dead or in prison. Some time had passed when Peter reappeared looking very smart and well. I asked,

"Peter, how long did you do in prison?"

"No, Tommy, I wasn't inside, I'm with a church. That's where I got my life back together." I thought,

'Is he serious, or is he off his head due to drugs?'

However, I didn't want to embarrass him so I said,

"Good luck, Peter."

"Jesus loves you and can change your life as well," he said.

"I don't think so, Peter. I've done too much and have hurt far too many people. He can't change this life that I'm living so there's no forgiveness for me." Peter left and returned a couple of weeks later and said,

"Tommy, I've got a friend who wants to meet you."

"What's he want to see me for?"

"He just wants to spend some time with you as I told him that you were a good friend of mine."

The people in my company advised me to have nothing to do with Peter as he may be working for the police. Something told me to take a chance, and that is what I did. On meeting Peter's friend, my first impression was that he leaned more towards a villain than Old Bill (the police). He had a big moustache and dark hair and introduced himself as Art. He told me he was from America and part of a ministry called Victory Outreach and came from a similar background to myself before being saved. Art revealed to me that he was once part of the Mexican mafia and a prison gang leader, where he ran the streets from his prison cell, and was also an assassin. To become a mafia member, Art had to prove that he had the bottle (guts), commitment and loyalty by murdering a rival gang member, which he achieved at 18 years old. Once Art was accepted into the mafia, he was told that the only way out was to die.

During a spell in prison, Art met someone who spoke to him about Jesus and his life changed dramatically and the mafia didn't go looking for him. Twenty-four years on, Art is an Evangelist and told me that Jesus could change my life. Out of respect for his past life, I just said,

"Art, that's good."

"Tommy, I want to tell you something but you may not understand it."

"What's that, Art?"

"Jesus said that you're the one." I frowned.

"I'm the one."

"Yes, Tommy. Can we meet up tomorrow?"

"Yes sure, Art."

For the next two weeks, Art would come to King's Cross, where we would talk over a coffee. On one particular day, Art came looking for me when I was on such a downer and I really didn't want anything to do with him. He told me,

"Jesus loves you."

"You keep telling me that but my life's the same and nothing is changing." I left King's Cross and returned to my flat in the East End.

I was in immense turmoil and pain and my mind was spinning non-stop with one hundred unsolved problems. The latest was that Nicky had given birth to our daughter, Justine. A normal father would be jubilant as it would be one of the happiest days of their life. However, all I could think of was that my little girl was going to die of H.I.V. and we had given her a death sentence. Although I moved out of the flat with Nicky during the pregnancy, as drug addicts, we needed each other. We were still friends and, even though I couldn't support her, I would visit her and also give her drugs, which wasn't a good thing, but that's what drug addicts do.

I sat on my bed in candlelight, feeling sorry for myself, with my drugs by my side, feeling sick and tired of the life that I was living. This was it; I mixed up the heroin and cocaine and put it into a syringe with tears flooding down my face thinking about my family finding me dead. It was the only way to get freedom from this lifestyle. I injected myself while sitting on the bed smoking a cigarette. I woke up on the floor with the needle snapped in my vein, where I must have fallen on it. My lit cigarette had fallen on to the bed but had gone out; I couldn't understand how it didn't burn the place down. I phoned my sister Maureen and told her,

"I have just tried to kill myself, and I couldn't even do that properly."

"Tommy, we've tried everything; what do you want us to do?"

61

"Please, take me back to that preacher in King's Cross," I begged.

My family came to my flat and took me to an address in King's Cross. It was 7 pm on the 13th of July 1993. Art and Pastor Bryan were there. I blurted out,

"I don't want to live this life anymore." Art replied,

"That's no problem." He said a prayer for me and asked me to repeat it, which I did; it was called The Sinner's Prayer. However, nothing changed; I was still feeling bad within myself. They asked me to go with them to a hostel, and as I was getting into a van with Art and Bryan, Ade, a friend of mine, approached me indicating for me to go with him to take some gear. I said,

"No, Ade, I'm going with these people. I've had enough."

"Going where? They can't help you," he said. I got into the van and we went to a place called the Lighthouse, a rehabilitation centre of the ministry for alcoholics and drug addicts. Art and Bryan assured me that Jesus was going to change my life. I just looked at them and thought, 'What am I doing here?' I was shown to my room which had two beds on opposite sides of the room. There was an Indian man lying on one of the beds and he introduced himself as Tony. We talked for a while before Tony shared his testimony with me. He had come to London with the intentions of becoming a successful chef, to enable him to send money back to his family for a better quality of life. However, Tony struggled and became an alcoholic and, at his lowest point, he could have died after setting fire to his flat. He was saved after his neighbours rescued him from the flames and brought him to safety. Tony was approached by Victory Outreach and given refuge in their recovery home, the Lighthouse, enabling him to get back on track with a trusting support system. Tony finished his testimony by saying,

"Tommy, Jesus can change your life like he's changed mine." Tony was one of the first people I connected with on the subject of Christianity.

I couldn't sleep thinking of the day ahead while contemplating leaving the hostel to get some drugs. I then thought of what Art had told me about Jesus and I said to myself, "Jesus, if you can change my life, I'll serve you for as long as I live."

In the morning, I went downstairs and had breakfast among the other residents. One of them asked,

"How do you feel this morning, Tommy?"

"Alright," I said.

"You don't feel sick?"

I thought about it and realised that I had just eaten a greasy breakfast and I felt OK when I was supposed to have felt ill. The director of the hostel suggested that I went for a walk with a man named John Blackshaw. As we walked around King's Cross, there were people calling me offering me drugs which I refused. On my return to the hostel, I met the Pastor, who said,

"Tommy, we would like to send you to a recovery home in America if you're to have any hope of getting your life back together." I wanted my life back and I wasn't feeling sick like I should have done so I agreed to go. That was the journey that changed the course of history in my life. After six months in Los Angeles in rehab, I was now feeling really good, just focusing on myself without anyone to distract me.

My new life in Christianity wasn't easy and a huge change to what I was used to, as I was addicted to the life of crime and drugs. I used to do things when I wanted to do them and say things when I wanted to say them. Christianity was a completely different discipline and mind-set; it is about being unselfish, caring, putting others first, educating yourself and having total trust and faith in God that things would work themselves out. I knew that it couldn't happen overnight so I had to take little steps each day to break the cycle. Many of my mentors were former villains and or drug addicts, which really helped me as they had natural empathy, understanding how I was feeling and thinking, as they had once been in a similar situation. They saw the good in me and were so non-judgemental, enabling me to open up to them in order to heal and grow. Knowing that my mentors understood the psychology of disenfranchised people like myself represented hope that I too could make it through.

Due to being so ashamed of being H.I.V. positive, I was in deep denial that I had contracted the virus and I never disclosed it to anybody. However, I now felt as though I was able to as I was in the right company, being among people I could trust, so I came clean to Pastor Bryan. I was constantly reminded by Pastor Bryan and Art that the same God who cured my drug addiction would cure my H.I.V. They sent me to get tested again, which I did, and the results confirmed that I was H.I.V. positive and that I couldn't be helped as it would soon develop to full-blown Aids. The church were praying for me. I was very upset and thinking of leaving the rehab as there was no cure, so no point, as I had no future. My Pastor asked me to have faith and that God would heal this and he assured me that they were all praying for me. On my return to hospital for another blood test, there was confusion with the results, and I was asked to have another test as they may have mistakenly had the wrong blood sample back. I took another test and returned for the results and walking into the hospital, I noticed that the team of medical staff were all looking at me in astonishment. I was then told that they couldn't find the virus in my blood and that they couldn't explain why. After retaking another blood test, the results were the same - H.I.V. negative - and they could not understand it, when they had medical evidence that I previously had been H.I.V. positive.

I fell on my knees in total joy and confusion, crying like a baby at the miraculous change in my fate. I felt like I had been given a pardon after being on death row. I had already come to terms with dying and now I had to re-think my future with the blessing of a new lease of life. I began to realise that God, through his son Jesus Christ, loves me and is a miracle-working God. This was unbelievable, as at the age of 44, I was ready to kill myself and now I have recently celebrated my 70th birthday. I thank God for my salvation and for my life.

I started travelling throughout the States, on crusades with my Christian family, to places such as Texas. It was an amazing experience seeing thousands of people from all walks of life attend, including gangsters and drug addicts. We put on dramas called The Duke of Hell 1&2, performed by people who were lost and now had their lives back. What really hit home was when I saw the gangsters and drug addicts go to the altar praying for change in their lives. I understood their struggles and I realised how fortunate I was to have this opportunity to change. Another crusade I went on was with an Evangelist and former gang leader from New York, Nicky Cruz, who became a born-again Christian in 1967. There was a book written about Nicky Cruz, 'The Cross and the Switch Blade' by David Wilkinson, who reached out to the gangs and the book was used in schools during religious education lessons in the 1970s and 1980s, and was also used in prisons. When the founder of the ministries, Pastor Sonny, first started ministering, he was demonised as the 'junkie preacher' and people thought no one would attend. However, 52 years on, there are over 600 ministries and recovery homes for men and women around the world run by young men and women who were just like Pastor Sonny; also lost. They have gone on to become licensed ministers. There was the pioneer generation, then the Joshua generation and now the third wave generation. There is also a food wave within the ministry; God is truly on the move in South Africa

It took about 2 years for it to really sink in and for me to accept that this is now my life. It is now 27 years since I gave myself to the Lord and I live my life according to the Bible. I have travelled to many places around the world, sharing my testimony; at the moment, I'm in Cape Town, South Africa, which is a war zone for gangsters and no different to the problems we face in London; just the location. I've been ministering in South Africa for over 12 years. We have a recovery home where I support families and have seen huge changes. We started a church in Cape Town, the Mother Church, and Pastor Sonny put together a group of ministers called team concepts whose aim was to develop Pastor Sonny's vision within the ministry. Within that time, 5 other churches were planted; one each in Mitchells Plane, Johannesburg, Eastern, Pretoria and Bloemfontein. They are all being run by ex-drug addicts and ex-gang members; God is certainly on the move in Cape Town, South Africa.

When I return to London, I reach out to people on the streets of King's Cross, one of my own haunts. Some of the old faces were at first amazed to see the new Tommy looking so happy, well and at peace with myself. Before long, they realised that I hadn't lost the plot and that I had really turned my life around. I now talk and pray for them which gives me so much joy and satisfaction, seeing them taking the steps leading to a more positive life. I am so grateful to be able to give something back, as I was given a second chance to be an example and not who I use to be.

My father hadn't spoken for years due to illness and we were told not to expect any improvement as he lay sick in hospital. I flew back from America to visit my dad, telling him about my new life as a Christian, excited like a schoolboy after his first day at school. With tears in my eyes, I asked him for forgiveness for all the stress and shame I had caused him over the years. My dad started talking to me and we continued like we never had before, seeing eye to eye for the first time. The doctors and my family couldn't believe it, seeing my dad in full flow dialogue with me after living in silence for so long. I think that my dad was waiting for me to turn my life around before he died. He wanted to see his eldest son capable of taking the reins of the family. It was then it dawned on me how strong my father was to tolerate all he did while holding down a job and bringing up nine children, clothing them and putting food on the table. I now understood why my dad sacrificed so much, because, if he had behaved as irresponsibly as myself and gone to prison, all his kids would have ended up in a children's home. Due to his love for his family, he took life on the chin. I now realised that my dad defined the true meaning of the term 'The Governor' and I never really was and didn't consider myself with that title like many people did, as people respected me for the wrong reasons. I was also forgiven by my mother who was very proud of me and she now felt able to talk about me to her friends, as I was reunited with my family in mind, body and soul.

Here I was, H.I.V positive, with my spiritual father, Art.

The King's Cross story 1993

My first son Jermyn & nephew Warren 1993

World conference 1993

Me and my sister Maureen 1993

Learning to be a father to my youngest son Clarke 1994

Pastor Bryan 1994

Getting ready for church 1994

1994 Graduating

The Duke of Hell play 1994

Testifying 1995

Evangelising 1995

800-mile charity bike ride 1995

The re-entry in King's Cross 1996

Sharing the word of God 1996

My church family 2017

My dad's funeral 1994

Me & Justine

My daughter Justine

My spiritual father, Art, 1998

Chapter 6.
The Grace and Forgiveness of God

Every couple of months, Art would come over to L.A. and spend time with me to encourage me as it wasn't an easy journey; it was a complete change of life. Being born again means you're literally innocent like a baby coming into this world with a clean slate, and the experience of life as a 44-year-old in my case. I had to adopt a new mindset, behaviour and habits, such as prayer, while giving myself to the Lord and maintaining total trust and faith that all will be well. Art was a fantastic mentor and spent 27 years as my spiritual father. Whilst in L.A., Art introduced me to his mentor when he first came into the ministry, who was an Evangelist Mondo (a senior). I was welcomed into his home amongst his wife and children and they became like family. I was really grateful to be part of the ministry which started in 1967.

In the early years, I had to confess not only about my H.I.V. but also that I was illiterate and couldn't read and write. I wanted to experience reading the Bible myself and not just being told about Jesus. Pastor Bryan referred me to Bible College which I attended for 3 years and, eventually, I was able to read and write. While reading the word of God, I came across a scripture, Ezekiel 36-37, which talks about Israelites who stayed away from God. Like me, I didn't know God and lived a dark life. God said to Ezekiel, "Go to Israel and tell them to change their wicked ways and I will take away their hearts of stone and give them a heart of flesh." That really rang a bell with me as my heart was black and stony. I knew that God was real and I continued to read the word of God. A passage that resonated with me was Mathew 8: 1-4 where there was a Leper who went to Jesus and said, "If it's your will, heal me," and Jesus healed the Leper. I was a modern-day Leper with H.I.V. So, if Jesus had done it 2,000 years ago, why not today? I minister the love of Jesus to anyone suffering from an addiction or sickness whenever the opportunity arises, and talk about the love of Jesus and forgiveness of sin.

While in the ministry, I received a phone call saying that my ex-girlfriend Nicky was in Chester and Westminster Hospital, asking whether I would go and see her. I met up with my daughter Justine who was now 18 years old and living in a children's home, and we went to visit Nicky who didn't look good and had lost a lot of weight. I greeted her with a kiss before being approached by the doctor, who told me that Nicky had full-blown Aids and she was dying. I was obviously sorry for Nicky and was still taken back by the news as it was now reality, although I wasn't surprised as it was to be expected. All I could do was be a comfort her. I took Nicky to the hairdressers to get her hair done, and spent as much time as I could at the hospital. I had, in the past, encouraged Nicky to give herself to the Lord like I had done and I ministered and prayed for her, and she went to the church on a few occasions and I know she felt the presence of the Holy Spirit, but just couldn't break away from that life. The next phone call I received told me that Nicky had died. At the cremation, Justine asked,

"Dad, why couldn't Mummy change like you?" I said,

"Justine, it was Mummy's choice just like it was my choice, and your mum didn't want to change."

Justine was devastated as she was very close to her mum. I loved Nicky and when I first met her, I wanted to take her away from that lifestyle. However, I was too wrapped up in my life as a villain and naively underestimated the power of that substance called heroin. Nicky died of a disease I was dying of and I believe, because I changed my life, God healed me and I know God would have also healed Nicky too. When Nicky died in hospital, Justine was there which had a massive impact on her and on myself as Justine really loved her mother. In the midst of Nicky's drug addiction, Justine witnessed everything she was doing and I was in prison at times, which was all very difficult for Justine to accept. Justine couldn't understand how God could save me and not her mother and, at that time, I didn't have the answers for her. If there was one woman who I could honestly say was the love of my life, it was Nicky. I was a criminal and Nicky was a drug addict and we met while both of us were in devastating circumstances and we supported each other in what way we could through our struggles. I miss Nicky so much and every time I see Justine, she reminds me of Nicky.

When people began to hear that I had become a Christian, they saw me as a Bible-basher who had lost it and had gone mad. However, I understood their attitudes, as it wasn't what we did; we weren't Christians - we were violent criminals and didn't believe in God. I would have reacted the same way before I gave my life to God. As the years went on, people would see me, on my return to London from America, looking well with a different attitude and persona and would ask, "Tommy, are you still in the church?" I would reply, "Yes," and they would laugh and wouldn't let me pray for them. However, 27 years on, I have friends who now send their children to me to pray for them, and people thanking me, saying, "You're such a blessing for the inspiration and encouragement you have given us. We believe in dead legends but you're a living legend, Tommy. Everyone in the East End knew of Tommy Jituboh as a villain and now we know you as a man of God." That's all I want; I don't want any accolades as I've had mine. God gave me my life back, so I just want to be an example to a family who has lost their son to prison, or a mother who may have lost her daughter to drug addiction.

I would like to be there for people, supporting them during their time of great need and it being known that I'm approachable to phone and for people to think, "Let me see what Tommy can do!" All I want is for people to think about what God has done for Tommy, a person who had no hope, and to see what my life was like, compared to where I'm at today. I would like to represent hope to those who believe there isn't any hope, as, if I can change, anyone can if they really want to. I'm now loving broken people, spending time supporting the recovery of drug addicts and praying for people around the world; that's the concept of the love of God that's offered to all of us - forgiveness. If we could only believe by faith, as it's only faith that will move the heart of God. It's not who I used to be, it's not my popularity, it's my surrendering to God and his forgiveness.

I was exposed to a lot of racism throughout my early years, especially with the National Front. There was also Mosley against the Jews, and in South Africa, there was apartheid and the jailing of Nelson Mandela for standing against it. There was the assassination of black leaders in America, such as Martin Luther King, who spoke out for equal rights. There was the rise of the Black Panthers who fought back against racism in the interest of the black communities. There was also race riots that swept across the country in the U.K. against racism and the police targeting black people. Did it have an effect on my life? I believe so. Did I become a racist? No, I didn't, I was just against injustice. If someone didn't like my colour and told me so, I would fight them; that's how it was - if you touch me, I'll touch you. If you said something wrong against me, you'd have to defend it. Growing up in the 70s I had a lot of white, Indian, Irish, African and West Indian friends; we were a mixed culture and we defended each other.

There was a football team from Wapping called the Jolly Sailor (the name of a local pub) who had a few half-caste and black players who were good players, such as Peter Tabi, Peter Jarvis, and Michael Mitchell and they all could have played professionally. When they played a team of dockers, they would be racially abused with taunts of, "Niggers", "Black b******s", "Coons" and "Jungle bunnies." However, they responded with their feet, giving them a lesson on how to play football, and they would never lose against the dockers who hated it. We were brought up not to respond to racial abuse, even though they would spit on my mother, calling her "Nigger Lover." And my dad would carry a knife to work for his own protection. My parents would always tell me, "Don't respond." Did it affect me when I saw how my parents were treated? You better believe it. But did it make me become a racist? No, it didn't. I just didn't like injustice, just like the government who put stipulations on me and I broke them.

Living the life of a high-ranking villain, I was privileged to hang out with famous musicians, for example, reggae superstars Gregory Isaacs and Dennis Brown. I was very good friends with them. I also knew Marvin Gaye who I met through his minder, Courbet, who looked after Marvin when he came to London. Marvin had a flat in Chelsea where we hung out at times. Although I personally lived a crazy lifestyle, I was exposed to a normality in other people's lives. The celebrities were intrigued with my life due to the influence I had on the night scene, however, I wasn't at all star-struck by their fame.

People from all spectrums of society knew me, from the highest to the lowest, and I was never in awe or looked down on people by how rich or poor they were. To me, money was for sharing and enjoying with people, and there was nothing more that I loved than taking scores of people from my community out on me. People would often come to me with their utility bills which they couldn't pay and eviction notices and ask me if I could loan them some money to keep a roof over their family's heads. I never once loaned them the money; I gave it to them from my heart. With the amount of cash I had at one point in my life, I could have become a loan shark earning bundles in interest. However, that wasn't how I thought or how I operated. I was a protector and stopped people from being bullied. Whether it was someone in high society who was owed money or a prostitute on the street who was taken advantage of by a pimp, I would deal with them.

When I reflect on my life, I know that it wasn't all bad; there was also good. However, now as a man of God, was I ashamed of it? Yes, I was, because I really hurt my family by the way I was living. If I could have changed things, I would have. I pray when this book is finished and people read it, they won't perceive my past as being exciting, but rather focus on the damage. I would be lying if I said that I didn't enjoy the feeling of the adrenaline high I received after getting away with cash from a robbery at that time of my life. It contributed to the swagger of arrogance of how I was regarded back then as The Governor. The image was just a mirage, as a governor doesn't traumatise people doing their everyday jobs. A governor is not violent and does not put their family through hell; it was all just an illusion. The lows by far outweighed any high and led to very dark places, such as 22 years in prison, drug addiction and the deadly disease H.I.V. and losing my family. The was nothing good I can say that came out of that life; that good happened only when I gave myself to Jesus and became a born-again

Christian. That's who I am today; I expose my testimony and share the loneliness and the damage it has done to my loved ones and myself. I am grateful for a second chance, as once, I was lost and now, I am found.

When I look back on my life, it really amazes me that I am still here at 70 years old, with the choices that I made and the things that I was committed to. I really believe it was the grace of God and my praying mother who would be on her knees in tears praying for my safety. I'm so grateful for my mother's unconditional love until the end, as I loved my mum so much. I'm now able to live as an example, not only to my grandchildren but to anyone stuck in a rabbit hole like I once was. Unknowing at the time, I was running away from my conscience, riddled with guilt from the hurt, pain and suffering I had caused people as a villain. I thought I could escape with heroin but I was wrong, as it took me to the brink of suicide. Every crime has a victim and, to be honest, I didn't give any of them a second thought at the time, as long as I got what I wanted. Through the grace of God, I have repented for over a quarter of a century and served the Lord supporting others and discouraging them from taking the same path as I did. The guidance of Jesus has enabled me to support many people turning their lives around and I shall continue to do so.

Running with my first gang at the age of seven, that was when I started to learn how to put on a different mask or a front and ignored my true feelings and emotions. Among my friends, I wanted to appear hard and regarded as the alpha male in the group. I became like a chameleon who could change my persona depending on who I came across, with my main focus not to show any weakness, as that's where my respect came from. Not being in touch with myself and hiding my true feelings had a detrimental effect on my life. I always felt an emptiness inside, whether I was alone or with a group of people, a void that was always there no matter how much drugs or money I had. I didn't know why I felt that way, or how to fill that void. When I was alone, I would then break down and cry, feeling sorry for myself, and often thinking about what advice my brother Robbie would have given me if he was still alive. Then my mates would knock on my door and I'd put that big smile on my face and play the character, while harbouring my true feelings.

Being a Christian enabled me to become a humane person, someone who's in touch with their feelings and not afraid to express them. I also now understand how to be true to myself in any environment and, unlike my previous life, I do not wear a mask, as Jesus has filled that void. It's been 27 years since a prayer changed the direction in which I was heading in. I now have a fulfilled life all due to someone spending time with me, believing in me and encouraging me, not just telling me what I wanted to hear, but telling me what I needed to hear, and for me to work it out. I now have something so precious in my life that no amount of money can buy - peace of mind.

My life changed so dramatically just from that simple belief in Jesus and helped to eradicate the addiction engrained into my DNA. I was someone who would be described as a character who had lost his life. However, I'm so grateful that the ministry that I'm now part of, Victory Outreach International, has given me an opportunity and trusted me with the ministry. Despite the life that I came from, they gave me the belief to enable me to go out into the world and share my testimony, and today, wherever the need is, I like to think that God would minister through my life. When I think about my lost, dysfunctional, violent and addictive life, I don't talk and point fingers at people, I point fingers at myself. I don't believe people have the right to point fingers at others as we don't know what they've gone through or what choices they had to make in dire situations. This will influence how they become the people they are; we don't know their circumstances.

I am grateful that I can stand on a platform, I can stand in a church, and I can stand in a football stadium and share my life with the world. Through the love of God, I hope to reach out to people who may be at the end of their tether with life and, through simple faith and belief in Jesus Christ, will show that we serve a miracle-working God. After all, what have they got to lose when there is so much more to gain? For over the last 10 years, I have been based in South Africa as that is where the direction of my life has taken me and where I have made a new family and spiritual friends.

I frequently visit London as I love it and I have my family there, although I do not miss it, as I'm on a new journey with Christ in my life. There is so much more need in other countries around the world where I would be far better served. Do I regret my life by the way it has turned out? Yes, I do, but not from the choices I've made, as I made those choices. I have regrets because I hurt my parents and my brothers and sisters. I have regrets because I hurt my parents and my brothers and sisters and I wasn't there to guide or protect my children. My sons, Jermyn and Clarke, were regarded as highly talented footballers and too good to be playing at an amateur level. They lacked that father figure to encourage them and take them for trials, training and cheering them on the touchline. If I had been there, my boys could have made it as professional footballers, as they had the ability. These are the areas I regret about my life. However, through the grace of God, I was able to get my life back before my parents died and received their forgiveness. My parents would be so proud if they were alive today and could see their bloodline prospering and breaking the cycle of my previous life.

I could have brought a curse onto my family, influencing my children or nephews or nieces through the life I was living. I thank God that they didn't follow my lead and I was able to pray for my grandchildren and pray for my cousins.

The only person able to help me with my life when I called for help was someone I couldn't see, named Jesus, and he has never let me down. Are there still challenges in my life? Yes, there are, and I believe that there are challenges in all of our lives, with drugs or without drugs, as life itself is a challenge; I realise that today. In Cape Town, I have a ministry called the Family Support Group where I'm working with between 60 & 70 families. I'm so grateful that I can now stand up and tell the truth, unafraid that I'll get found out by a lie, as the truth will set you free.

Sometimes in life, you can miss an opportunity that you regret and, before you know it, it's gone by you and that's exactly how I felt regarding my children. I brought them into the world but I wasn't a father due to the dysfunctional choices I made, so I never raised them. I wasn't there for them or featured in their lives while they were growing up. However, when I gave myself to Jesus on the 13th July 1993, during the process of rebuilding my life as a human being, a Christian and a man of God, it led me to the path of hope and faith enabling me to rekindle my relationship with my children. Over the last 28 years, my children, Jermyn, Clark and Justine, have all accepted me as a father in their lives. Jermyn, my eldest son, has four children and where I missed out on being a father to my kids, I am now able to be a father to my grandchildren, Gracie, Marley, Dolce and Jersey. My second son, Clarke, has a daughter, Amelia, and Justine hasn't any children at present. I am grateful for this second chance in my life, experiencing fatherhood as a grandad, which was only possible through God, the people that have been in my life since it changed, and the fellowship that took me in, allowing me into their lives and being around their children and experiencing holding a new-born baby which I lost sight of when my children were born. It's a great feeling and I want to encourage people reading this book who may be, for whatever reason, estranged from their children. God can change your life as he did mine.

That feeling when your children have forgiven you for not being a father in their lives is a tremendous experience that will always stay with me. When my son Jermyn said to me, "Dad, I love you and I forgive you," It broke me and since I've become a Christian, I've been able to pray for my son. Jermyn can now come to me as his father with any issue and I can now support Jermyn over any hurdle, which was only possible by having Christ in my life. Now that my children have seen the change in my life over a period of time, they realise that they have their dad back and now trust that I'll always be there. This is not about me but having Christ in me as I can now give positive direction to my children which I never could before.

In the 27 years since giving my life to Jesus, I have been on a tremendous journey through faith. I've been invited to different countries to talk in churches. In London, during my previous life, no one would really trust me as, once they heard my name, they just thought of badness. However, when I now revisit the U.K to see my family, I've been invited to schools to give talks and to churches to speak at services. I'm so grateful that, at the age of 44, when I was thinking of committing suicide, and on the 13th July 1993, Jesus saved my life. Now, in 2020, I'm doing what I really believed I was called to do - going into the world with God's forgiveness and love which I will continue to do until the Lord takes me home. I will share the gospel, as once, I was lost but through the grace of God, I was able to find my way home. To God be the glory.

Since I have been in London during this lockdown due to the Coronavirus pandemic, I have been inundated with calls from people from Africa and London who have referred people to me for a listening ear. Many were from parents with sons and daughters or nephews or nieces who were struggling with their lives. Many people became aware of my natural ability to reach out to people and I have gained a good reputation over the 27-year period since being saved myself. Many of those who contacted me were people who I would have never associated with before I was found because of the type of person I was. It took many years before I was taken seriously, as in the early days, people would say, "Tommy, a Christian? He'll rob the church, just wait and see. He's not no Christian, he's a lunatic." As the years have passed, they say, "Tommy, you really have changed and I can see that you are a man of God. We've heard so many good things about the work that you've been doing around the world." These are the phone calls I'm now getting from the same people who would have avoided me 27 years ago.

Twenty-seven years ago, there was a phenomenal moment that changed the direction of my life for the greater good, a prayer that brought Jesus into my life. I would like to give you the opportunity; if you are lost in yourself and struggling with your life, just repeat this prayer:

"Lord Jesus, I am a sinner and I ask for your forgiveness. I believe with all of my heart that you are the son of God and you died for me and, on the third day, you rose to give me a new life. I confess with my mouth and I believe with my heart that you are the son of God in Jesus' name. Amen."

If you have said this prayer, I would encourage you to get in touch with a church and let them know that you would like to become part of the church. If you would like to get in touch with me, I'll leave my details at the end of the book.

God bless you.

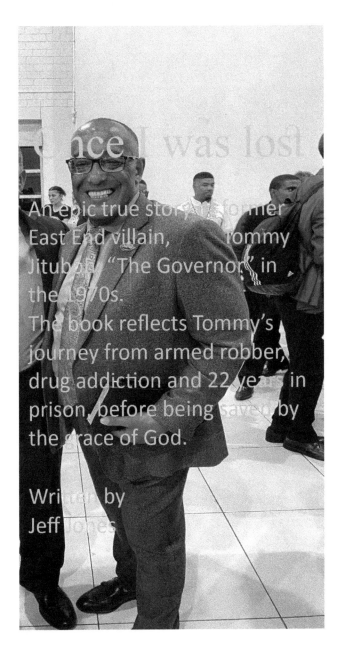

Once I was lost

An epic true story of former East End villain, Tommy Jitubony "The Governor" in the 1970s.
The book reflects Tommy's journey from armed robber, drug addiction and 22 years in prison, before being saved by the grace of God.

Written by
Jeff Jones